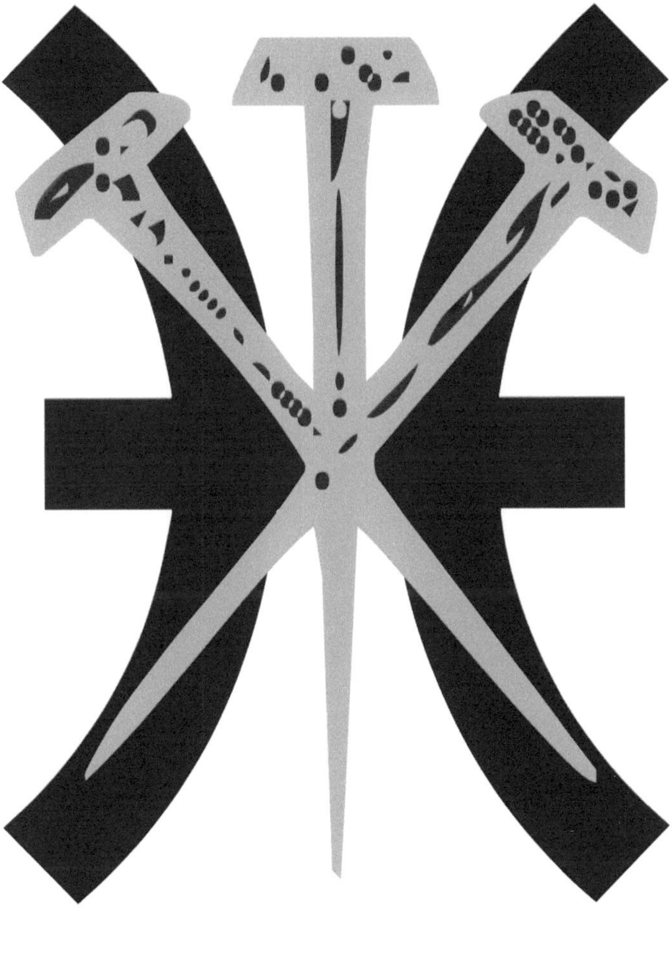

INK SPILLS
AND FIVE NOTES OF SUICIDE
DOMINIC LYNE

Published by **Degraded Discord**
an imprint of **DPL Publishing**, 2010

www.dom-lyne.co.uk

Text copyright © Dominic Lyne, 2010

The Author asserts the moral right to be identified as the author of this work.

Cover design and layout by Dominic Lyne © 2010

Pisces Nails logo is copyright © ***DPL Publishing***, *2007*

All Rights Reserved.

No part of this publication may be reproduced, stored in a retrieval system, or transmitted in any form by means, electronic, mechanical, photocopy, recording or otherwise, without prior permission of the publisher.

The views expressed in this book are not necessarily those of the publisher.

ISBN: 978-0-9561612-1-5

This is not for you.
But it is for *you*.

FIVE CIGARETTES

Else these are my final moments.

I stand in the doorway. Everything is as it always is in the tomb of my memories. Love existed when we arrived that first night with the keys in front of it on the wooden floor, drinking microwaved tea from my feet.

I work a cigarette into my ghosts, my memories. I wipe my face. Stupid tears, what shaking hands. Welcome to this moment, sorry for its lack of glass. One more drag and it reaches its end. I flick it out onto the television screen. Conversations gave way to cold silences, unknown. 'This, whatever it is, is more perfect.'

Cut the scene to a few hours later. Returning from having a cigarette to find him sat there, face covered in entwined sleep. The tear falls down my cheek slowly. It's my final middle finger, a lingering element of my part in the relationship. People, when you stop growing you start rotting. The fireplace voice echoing around the vacant space. So this is a smile? A memory. Melt away all the furniture to the shell, nothing lasts forever, that's why I'm sat here, alone, shaking. Click, flame, inhale. Another cigarette breathes to life in my sunlight. No, it couldn't be no, life has proved all too well that that is just a lie. I guess you stop growing as my mouth. I'm not allowed to smoke inside the room, it doesn't belong to me anymore; it belongs to the feet, that was all we had.

Ten months later. The same room, the

cigarette breathes its last and stumbles to the floor to be reanimated by a drop of love. There is no fairytale though, they've walked this path so many times that now its enjoyment and damage mean the things that indicated my existence. I once believed that love could last forever. I loved him you know. Certain are we? That's where trust comes in. Long story short, forgotten and only the silence remains in its wake. I sigh. I smile coldly. How like the past year, ignited with a final look around. This is just the end of a chapter.

Guess he loved me; he said he did but we never truly know for same voice is now devoid of warmth. He opened one door; I opened another. I wipe my face. I sigh. Image, him stood there by the coal, us snuggled in the television screen. When I was young, I once believed that love could last forever. Smile.

Back in the present, this is the end of the countdown. Those days, what good will they do? There's no magic garden under my feet. A cigarette breathes its last and stumbles to the floor to where arguments existed here. It couldn't be the vision in your head devoid of anything that belongs to me.

A lingering hour.

I throw a cigarette into the balcony before me and watch its dying gasps against the solid scent of you. The cigarette dies slowly, our relationship rotted within these four walls. It's somewhere.

BOOK ONE
FIFTY INK SPILLS

00

Maybe we need an introduction. Maybe not. Does a reality exist anywhere? Do I really need to give some form of history of my life? Does everything require a fucking back-story? Blah blah. 'Characters need a past in order for the reader to get a feel of what is happening, to form a context.' BOLLOCKS. You're dealing with my present so deal with it dear reader. All you need to know is that I'm here. Here because one fucking decision I made was the wrong one and now I gotta deal with all the shit. So yeah, this might feel like a lemon squeeze on your brain but hey, that's just the way I roll baby. Guess we need to define the outlines before we go on.

This isn't some self-help psychobabble tale of woe-is-me proportions. This isn't some cry for help. This is just it, as it is, and with no philosophical explanations on what *it* actually is. This is a moment, a part, a passing. Movement from one place to another without barriers. If I fuck you'll know about it. If I fantasise it's here too. If I choose to die, well that'll be… that won't be here, it's not an option.

So here's the deal, I'm letting you guys into my head. That's it, that's all you're getting. Part of a story, my waking thoughts and you need to fill in the blanks with your own opinions. Work out in your head what's going on. Create a vision of my life. Try and find a real me, and in doing so you might understand something new about yourself. Who knows, actually, who the fuck cares? I got my own impressions to deal with.

This is the output of fifty mornings. Fifty ink spills across blank pages of a book. Fifty waking thoughts scrawled through half open eyes. Fifty mornings getting over *him*.

So, sit back, kick your feet up and get tissues ready – for reasons that may not be the obvious. Welcome into my head, both of them.

01

Alarm. Broken faces and shattered minds. People's lives existing for but a moment. A world of dreams forgotten in an instant. Our minds spend eight hours existing somewhere else. Its own hidden world.

Darkened leaves fall from trees like brittle spectres, another year dying, crumbling from existence. We'll never have those days again. Such is life.

I guess I heard him say it. How insignificant it all is. He didn't really say it unless our minds connected on some subconscious level and dropped nuggets of venom like atom bombs. Melting and destroying everything within a split second, leaving our waking mind with the aftershocks.

Dead man coughs and the world shimmers. Gypsy queens in the dead of night, legs folded like forbidden prostitutes.

I bet I look like shit.

Fat walrus cums with a roar. Shoots cum over its matted black fur. Over the top noise for pathetic sex. My dick never grew so small, totally and utterly turned off. Bit of sick in my throat, can't swallow given the amount of saliva the walrus generates in what it perceives as a kiss. Spit when it goes down to try and breathe some life into my cock. Fuck, I must look so bored. Closed eyes turn him into Adonis for one second before the image fades back to reality. Bestiality. Shudder. Self punishment, self torture. Equate sex to some of the most disturbing moments.

I'm like a fantasy to them. At least they got something out of it. I really should charge again, that way it wouldn't seem so empty, so pointless, so undeserved.

Yes, yes, yes, yes, yes… no!

Memory.

'Look what you do to me. Let's have sex.' 'Okay.' And that was the start of it all. Well, not the start. The commitment, the uncaring change over. Fuck the future then text the present whilst the past is waiting to hear from you.

02

Which one has a small? So hung-over this is gonna be shit. Definitely know I look like crap today.

Life injured, taken outside, welcome to London I guess, could have happened anywhere. Fuck, so so drunk. A little disappointed, well not a little, a lot but that I won't write about. Shit happens.

When the nightmare is over the children sleep. It's a pain but what about adult nightmares?

Dream, dream, place everything in a waking dream.
Fuck. I need to get up.
    Bastards.

03

Shadows fall; a world turns in a void of silence. A mother cries as father walks out of the house, baby oblivious in the cot.

Nothing lasts forever, so many stories tell us that. Everything changes each and every day, there is nothing you can do or say to change that fact. But who really wants anything to last forever?

Happy smiley face, big toothy grin. Kick back, kick back to let the sun right in. Warm the soul in its rays and remember everything is good. Dissatisfaction is just a key for which we need to find a lock. Open up a Pandora's Box and fill the world with new diseases. Doors open, doors shut. Life is like a big old mansion, dusty and full of memories, some on display, others locked away and hidden within the fabric of the walls.

If only we could remember all our dreams. That would make for some fucked up reading. I wonder sometimes if I do actually just go wandering around like Tyler Durden in *Fight Club*. Living this other life and one day I'll wake up and see it. Everything will crumble and I'll be like 'what the fuck?' Would everything then make sense? I dunno. Maybe.

Would explain a lot I guess.

04

Toss and turn, toss and turn. I can't sleep when there's someone else in my bed. Always nicer to sleep alone.

    Still so so tired. Just wanna lay in bed all day.

    'A few more years, a few more wrinkles.'

    Vague hand wobbling off into ink trail. God, why can't I remember my dreams?

Sorry, fell back asleep. Guess I'll get the hang of this soon.

A three legged dog whimpers at a half moon in the sleet. There's something incomplete with that image.

05

Too hung-over, trailing room from room like a zombie. Half dead. I'm gonna be good this weekend I reckon. Just a few drinks tonight. Eep, *he'll* be there and hopefully not with the brown shit.

Dream version we had a talk and I was strong and unyielding, if only that was how it ran in life. Blah. I'll shake and feel 'argh' like some stupid little girl. Haha. Okay, kinda.

Oh, it was confirmed last night that that time in the pub when all the market people were around, we kissed, and no one saw us haha.

'I'm sure we kissed that time?'

'We did.'

'Oh good, I just didn't want to think it was some weird fantasy.'

06

'You left without a word.' Of course I did, do you think you deserve better?

Big red eyes, no one makes me cry. Bully bully, everyone picking on me. You can all fuck off. Fuck off all of you. One law for them another for me. Why is that the case? Two-faced wankers locked in their bitter lives of lies and deceit. Delusions of grandeur. You're nothing but market traders for fuck-sake. You're not anything special at all.

I am not scared of you. I am not nor will I ever be.

God I feel like shit. Yes, hung-over again. It's kinda habit now.

'Do you think I'm putting my life on hold?' Of course not, when did you ever do that for anyone? It can bring the ex and everyone is happy and 'woo', I turn up with someone and I'm the devil in a human form. My horns hidden under my cap. Wankers. Fucking wankers.

I'm gonna look like shit. Big puffy cry eyes and dry skin. Body in a constant state of atrophy. A look in the mirror. Confirmed. Got a cut on my cheek. Cheers, dunno how I got it. I don't feel bad about last night at all. I held no punches. Hold it against me if it keeps you warm. Like I said, everything changes.

Anyway, this is starting to sound like a proper fucking diary. Eep.

07

This has become all a bit tiresome. Not the writing just my inability to sleep again. I wanna dream dreams, not keep reliving something that's already happened. Maybe because it's fresh, its aftershocks linger but fuck, some days I simply wish I wasn't me you know.

If I could walk a waking dream then I would. These stupid realities where I think I've achieved so much then I re-awake and am like 'oh' so I didn't get that e-mail, that call never happened. Maybe I'm going insane or need to get out of my own mind for a while.

Always trusting the bad apples. Always getting used and let down. At some point I think I'll just vanish.

Sounds like the fucking Martians have arrived outside. Rhythmic metallic grindings; rise, fall, hit the ground, rise, fall, hit the ground.

Feel a bit sick. I think it's coz I'm cold. Guess winter is finally rolling in. Christmas is just around the corner. Then wow, another New Year. Rolling on. Spinning towards destruction daily. How can something be so mundane and monotonous, yet completely different? I got the Meatloaf lyrics in my head. 'Life is a lemon and I want my money back.'

08

So hard to get out of bed today. Alarm went off at 8. It's now 10. Maybe I needed the sleep.

I can see the rain against the window. It's rained for two days. I can hear it falling onto the street below. Got to go out in it. Blurgh! Weird how the rain changes the everyday sounds around you. The cars sound different, more distant. Muffled. A competition for dominance.

I should get up. I'm still not used to being alone.

I always fear the first daily glance into the mirror. I fear it more than the final one.

From where I'm standing it looks like you're playing dirty. You say one thing then do another, the famous double standards. You will always be too selfish to ever see any wrong doings in your actions, the scary thing is you delude yourself and carry on with your reckless pride. You say you loved me but it was far from PURE and SIMPLE and definitely not SELFLESS. You wanted control and the frightening thing is you still want control even now.

You judge everyone on appearance including my friends. You are even more fucked up than [name omitted] because as least he could see his faults and 'til this day tries to be a better person.

Oh leave me the fuck alone. Stop trying to put me down even after we've parted ways. Listen, can't you hear it? No? Exactly, that's the silence my love's become.

09

More confused dreams. Am I awake or not? Scared, maybe I do have a double life.

Sleepy, sleepy. Got to go to work though. Blurgh. Things get sorted, everything returns to normal. Well, some things you don't get but they are obviously not meant to be.

Touch my soul and tell me what you feel. Is it warm or cold? Place your hands upon it and heal its weeping sores. I wish, yeah I wish. No one could ever do that. It bleeds, a trail of blood like a ribbon behind me, splattered along the path of my past. You can always see where I've been.

Outside a girl's crying on the phone. I wonder what news she's received. Bad news, a break up, death? 'We could just meet up for a drink?'

Funny that for this moment her life has crossed mine and yet she means nothing to me.

Die die fuckers, die. Yeah that's what I wanna say. Die die fuckers, die. Taste my fist.

Fist fuck, face fuck, cock suck, ass lick. Bare back, cum shot. Shit out sperm.

10

I'm a little bit crazy, just a bit strange. Got a pocket filled with pennies because the pounds got spent away. My fingers smell like bleach, but that might just be cum from last night. Yeah, who knows, yeah who knows? Most likely anyway.

Happy and kinda sorted now. Well for the most part anyways. Just need a few more dreams to come true and that'll be good. Haha. Not so sleepy this morning. Gotta get up. Got to go to the gym.

Why did I get black bed sheets? You can see the sex upon them, like tale-tale marks of debauchery. Yeah, maybe I should have got a paler colour. Not to worry though.

Back to black or black to back. Ha, who said the brain works so well all the time? I can hear a motorbike, a bus, a car, a police siren. If I go and open my window I'll hear people. Living people. Market people. Living in the middle of a soap opera. Dirty me, the villain of the piece. I am quite bad when I'm single. Come to think of it, I'm quite bad when I'm not.

Me, piggy. Right, crawling out of bed now to face the new day.

11

When did waking up become so much effort? Coldness of winter I guess. Not to worry, cold makes you appreciate the warm shower I guess. Dearie me, I just wanna lay all snug for the whole day but alas, once again I have to jump out and get up.

    Alarm goes off for the third time. Reset each time manually. No snooze button here.

Shut the real world out. Shut the real world out. Escape into fiction and just write away the soul. Bugger piss flaps. I gotta sit outside all day. Shit. Fuck. I might go for some thermals. Yay, get me. Oh bugger, time to start being suffocated by your own clothes. I wonder what'll happen today? Maybe an actionscript wank, a conversation with a corpse, get shouted at by an Italian woman, or asked to make zombie porn. Maybe all of the above.

Right my sorry ass, you are getting out of bed right now.

12

Silent morbidity. Dunno, everything goes I guess. Try to think positive about everything but it's not always that easy. Some things are just not meant to be I guess.

Memory.

His stupid face popping up from the other side of the counter and saying 'I love you' for the first unexpected time. All gone now.

Present.

A new face, new person. What if he's getting too into me, like proper? Am I leading him on? Can I be accused of doing that? Do I really wanna get sucked into something now, when the present is still such an un-healing mess?

How long do cuts take to heal mother? It depends child, just don't pick at the scabs to see what's beneath. Lies, lies, lies. I just wanna see beyond the fucking horizon.

Mama said, mama said, I can't even remember what mama said. Just close your eyes. Close them and see where the vision takes you. Walk blind, your little white stick tapping away against the ground, a slow and useless movement with no surroundings to appreciate visually.

If you sleep in a memory, you might wake up to a truth.

He stubbed his toe, which caused a blood clot, which ended up in his brain. That's a pretty lame way to die.

I hate the struggle between dreaming and consciousness. Feels like a war to stay on one side of the mirror. Maybe that's what we all want; the whole of mankind just laid on its back sleeping. Think how peaceful the world would be if that happened. No wars, no violence or death; no love, no random acts of kindness. The world would just turn in silence on its yearly round trip around the sun.

The void.

Fuck, I do need to eat something healthy at some point. I've been drinking every day this week. So many pints of Fosters. Fuck, who cares?

13

Another morning, another day. So what will I achieve today? Probably nothing, who knows? Just wander forward and see what happens I'm guessing.

Hello world, hello big swirling ball of mud, rock and magma. What if we are the only life in the universe? Just a blip, a mistake in the void. Alone, screaming at the darkness around us. Evolved bacteria.

God, he's so fucking lazy, so conceited. Channelling up his own ass at the rate of MPH. Arrogance ain't pretty nor is constant vanity. Click, click, camera flash. Self absorbed, clinging on for little more than self-punishment. Get over it. Get over it for fuck-sake.

Crippled child walks, his face like Butterball. Big fat dangling lip and overgrown face. Almost something John Merrick about him, but yet he is surrounded by girls. Guess you need a deformity these days to get any luck in that department. Pity the new lust; ugly the new beauty. Forgive me as I rush to be sick.

'You judge everyone on appearance.' So what, big fucking deal. Who doesn't? Blame, blame, blame. Just accept your guilt and deal with it. I really don't fucking care at the moment.

Warmth, we all require warmth, be it warmth of comfort or warmth of the soul. The cold makes us unhappy. Lately each morning I just want to stay in bed. I really should get back into my old habits of jumping up and getting on. But it's autumn; all I want to do is hibernate until the spring. Ha, I fucking wish.

Be a bear curled in his cage peacefully. How the fuck do they manage to sleep for so long? Fuck knows.

14

Eyes open, once again I want to lay here. I wish I was in the arms of someone I loved but I'm not obviously. Monday, lazy day. Guess Mondays are my Saturdays or Sundays. I just like to do nothing on them.

Freedom and love. That's it. Freedom and love.

Dozed off again. Whoops. Day passing by and I'm still here. Same bed. Am I getting lazy? Nah, just relaxing. De-stressing. Boring.

Grumble, grumble, grumble, grumble. I just wanna remember my dreams. Smack! Have them hit me full pelt in the face like that.

I remember an old man, topless, leering in through a window. The snow falling around him, settling within the wrinkles of his skin. I closed the curtains on him and returned to the open fire.

Saw Steve yesterday, was nice. One of the lucky ones who got away. Dated him when she died. He was there for me at that time. But then I met someone else. You can't help wondering what would have happened if I'd turned the other way, especially given where my choice has taken me. That ain't regret, it's just a ponder. I guess I would have ended up somewhere. Most likely nothing would have changed.

I can't complain, no, I can't complain about any of this. What would be the point? I sleep in a whisper. I age in a dream.

If I die today with a penny on my eye can I go there and kiss this world goodbye?

15

Those dreams got scary last night. Really didn't know if I'd wrote some stuff or not. I got really 'argh' and frustrated. Almost crawled out of bed to check. Not good. I just want peace of fucking mind. Not these stupid fucking dreams.

16

A throat like a bullfrog.

Don't stay out late on a school night. Haha. Where's Wally? Guy at the bar with his notebook scratching away. Me just a cold bitch.

Grumpy woman in the Diner, they're never happy there. Never smile, just slam food down, whisk it away. Eye force you out. Ha. Food ain't that great, nor is the beer. 'Tastes like kiddy beer.'

'Who wants to spend the night with each other raise a hand… okay, the question is where?'

Back to mine. Once again I'm laid here stinking of cum. Bed sheets just get dirtier.

Fucking elephant trunk.

I should really wash them but I'm working this week so they'll have to wait.

Moral of the story? What I said at the start. Don't stay out late on a school night.

17

I've always been just that little bit delayed, even though I'm usually early and on time.

It's definitely that time of year when you don't want to get out of bed and into the cold. Brr, got to do it though, even if you have nothing to do!

Just wanna relax with nothing on my mind but there is always something bugging me, always some little negative or unresolved issue chewing away in that head of mine. At least I slept last night. I think…

If we could sleep for a thousand years, what sights would we see? Would we become so accustomed to living in our dreams that the reality we awake into would be just mere fantasy? Would we be happier in our land of fiction, rather than have to learn the new ways of the future?

Are the dead content as they sleep in their dreamless slumber?

So much time wasted through neglect and fear, and yet you could still put in all the effort you can and still get nowhere. Struggle, struggle, fucking struggle.

What will I be doing today? Wank, shower, work, read, sell a few things hopefully, read, eat, smoke, home, eat, read, write, wank, sleep. Woo, great fun.

Dissatisfaction is the keystone of my life.

18

Good morning again. Why does time go so quickly when it is dreamed away, yet so slow when lived? I need to create a regime, well maybe not but I should kick myself into focus, I don't wanna be like Kafka, famous post-life with a series of incomplete novels. Buckle down boy and get to it. Otherwise I'll get stuck in a rutt – ha RUTT, how bout that for something destined to go nowhere?

Only short one today, there is nothing going on inside this head of mine. Just the typical worries and shit. Like I've always said, one day I'm gonna be truly happy, it just won't be whilst I'm young.

I don't want to get too old though. The longer you are alive, the uglier you become. It's like watching your body decay in front of your own eyes. Maybe it's so gradual that you don't notice. I don't wanna find out to be perfectly honest.

10:12. Guess that means I should get the fuck out of bed. Lazy week this one with no gym and all that. That *will* change next week; I might be daring and go three times. Don't hold me to that.

19

Missed a day, was having sex, sorry. Bed sheets really need to get washed now. Cum marks everywhere.

Flat's a mess, clothes and shit everywhere. Typical me I guess; will tidy later. Last day of work until Wednesday. Wonder if it'll be busy.

I'm a cunt apparently. Think I can live with that.

One day I'll scar this world with my writing. Hopefully leave one big rip right across it. I've left a mark wherever I've gone, so I really wanna leave one here.

This is my world and it's filled with darkness. This is my world and I wanna nuke it with an atom bomb. Let it explode and watch the dust fall like snow, blackened by all the experiences and letdowns I've had.

You can't look me in the eye. Let's be honest. You threw away love for the freedom to fuck around. Good for you cupcake. Good for you.

Looks like I'm gonna wear thermals today. Woo. Fucking winter.

20

Yay, hung-over again. Go me. There's just a mass of clothes on the floor. Should be scoring some K tonight. 2grams of the stuff. That will be fucking sweet as. That'll be fun. Get me high, get me high, get me so fucking high that I hit the sky. Then I'll fall back down. Lay around. The high, high, high I go. Disassociate me from this world so I can see how it works, and be even more disgusted.

The iPerson Touch. Can't be bought new and has previous owners. Limited life span and will not be yours forever. May have been used by more than one person at a given time. No guarantees or refunds offered.

Right, should really get up. Got things to do and sort out. I just wanna stay in bed again. I can see today being a lazy day. Real lazy.

21

I could achieve so much more if I wasn't so lethargic. The cold puts me off I guess, would rather be wrapped up warm inside than pissing ice cubes.

Had another date last night. He was really sweet. Nervous tremors and hand movements. I was smitten by it all. Made me smile. I guess I'm a man whore now. Ha, no, I'm not that bad.

So Mr Sleepy, what shall we do? Get up, get up, drag ourselves out to do something. Gym boy, gym boy. Let's wake ourselves up with weights.

Ragh. Argh. Blurgh.

If I could wait for just one minute would the course of history be changed? Who knows, every second causes a different alternative, all dying and collapsing in on themselves.

He was so sweet; nervousness is something attractive. Hmm. We'll see. I reckon I could. Let's see how everything pans out. Someone will get hurt but such is this world.

Fuck, I really am a cunt.

22

'Good morning good sir, would you like a punch?'

'Why, that would be wonderful.'

PUNCH.

'How was that?'

'Jolly good.'

The air is so cold, vicious wraith-like fingers caressing you, wrapping phantom arms around you as they drag you to hell.

Alarm, alarm. Fuck off alarm. Is this how wage whores feel as they search for money everyday? Yes, this is a taste of the world I want to escape. Money, money. If only it grew on trees in summer so we could sleep all through winter. Other animals exist without it, why can't we?

Hey sick feeling, fuck off. I will not be ill.

Slack ass whore with no arse. Just a tunnel at the top of legs. Gaping chasm for cock. Wanting, seeking, waiting to be penetrated. Man after man falling through like trains through a tunnel. Cock cums into latex, the other spurts across a barren desert, white patches against tanned flesh.

In the valley of the dead, only the lies have eyes. Souls long since departed. Searching to fill the vacuum with anything that creates an illusion of completeness. If you die with no soul there's nowhere for you to go. Body just rots, that slackened ass crack fades to dust, the pleasures it supplied forgotten and now useless.

This is the kiss of death, the moment of conception. Two cells merge. New life, the beginning of decay. The gift of what we become is the promise of where we end.

At the end of it all, we are all forgettable.

23

Wake up minute before the alarm goes off. Stayed in bed, makes sense to catch up on sleep you've missed.

Only three more mornings of this then back to usual. The lay-ins without care.

Sleepy, tired, fall down and be awoken by a kiss. A sleeping beauty. Yeah right.

Shower time, clean the skin, wash away all the dirt from yesterday and leave feeling refreshed. If only everything was that simple.

I guess I really shouldn't start a working day with a line of K.

24

'How you doing?... I'm cool... Good to see you again... Yeah okay... Catch you soon.' Hearing one side of a conversation is funny. Only get half the facts.

Half... half awake, half asleep; half lived and half dead. Count down from 100 and see how far you get. I normally just forget where I was and have to retrace my steps.

Twelve grabbing hands reaching out to grab you, to pull you under when you least expect it... wait, déjà-vu. Could I be thinking the same thing again at the same moment? Haha, I almost wrote 'finking'.

Deadlines, deadlines. I hate fucking deadlines. They couldn't give it a nicer name. How are you meant to get excited by something so morbid?

My eye caught my neon DCs, so bright against everything else in the room. I wanna be a bright star, shining out and drawing attention. People just looking without knowing why.

'There's something about him, I don't know what.' That's what the mother had said. 666 burnt onto my scalp. I'll stick a needle through your damaged windpipe. You wheeze a lot of dead air anyway.

Everyone seems to be dying this year. 2009 is a year of death. I'm at the age now where I work towards being alone from all those who were there as I grew into what I've become.

What the fuck have I become?

Lanky guy gets cramp because his Empire State Building sucks all the blood away from his legs. Pointing to the heavens with its steel capped beacon. Tries to force itself into the small crater of the moon. Doesn't fit so it erupts like a volcano, spitting down cooling lava against a floor of flesh.

25

One-armed bandit, dead of night, shattered glass and fingers off ice.

Blind man ejaculates across the face of his lover, walking stick squeezed up his ass, its white stained with shit. Lover pulls it out and licks it, shoots off a load on useless eyes.

Naked flesh glistening with sweat. Two people entwined. Wrapped around each other like coiled snakes, biting and kissing. Penis erect and firm, digging warmly into closed skin, seeking a warm hole.

I will suck you dry. Feel the cum hit the back of my throat and swallow. The throb of your cock in my mouth.

When you cum over me, the chances are that someone is dying in the world.

26

Screech, bang, clatter. The sound of knives being dragged across the floor. Devils on people's backs, their claws dug deep into flesh. Hardwired by hate, consumed by greed. Who gives a fuck about anyone else these days? Everyone seems so self-serving and empty.

Darkened alleys hide their threats in shadows, long dark fingers waiting to catch you off guard. Maybe, maybe, what? Lost it… dead.

Why don't you hurry up and die? So I can go to your funeral and piss on your grave. Leave a big rancid puddle by your head, watch the weeds grow as your twisted body is eaten away by worms. Rotting flesh. We all rot down there.

I wish, I wish for… what do I wish for? A lot but nothing ever goes my way. Some people get everything. I just struggle, struggle, fucking struggle and what do I have to show for it? Nothing. Absolutely fucking nothing. Nobody wants me in any shape or form. If I dropped dead today, who would actually notice?

Today's the day my future phone call was made. The static on the line. Something could happen today but then again, I doubt it.

27

Black eyes stare out of hollow sockets. Bile running from the mouth, yellow orange. Figure stumbles forward a few steps before collapsing to the ground in a mouldy heap.

Crash, roll, bang; crash, roll, bang. Crash, roll, slide, bang. Crash, roll, slide, bang, laughter. The noises of life filtering up from the street.

What have you seen throughout your existence? Buildings like silent sentinels, memories locked both inside and out. Happiness, rage, despair and love all absorbed within the bricks and mortar.

Throat like an ashtray. Tastes stale. 'I'll never smoke, such a filthy habit.' Yeah fucking right. Fingers tainted, nose bitter with the drugs from the night before. So maybe I'm happy. What would I be without my powders and plants? What would I be?

I'm dying, rotting to the earth. Settled in my loneliness. Living alone, rattling around the flat. So glad it isn't any bigger. I'd go insane.

28

Soft off.

    Arms gripped and legs held apart. Hand grabs at cock. Ejaculate in boxers. Released.

    Pulled into a ball, legs apart, dick against ass, felt through the fabric. Cock cums, sprays over the ass. Released.

29

Old habits die hard, I guess that's what makes them that.

Whilst his cock is in my ass he starts speaking Spanish.

'Wot?'

Ass in face, the musty smell seeping out. Ass, cock and balls all within reach of one tongue trail. Fingers into mouth and hand rubbed across face, I didn't quite get it. Whatever turns you on.

With dick up the ass, piss warm over the chest, raining down upon him like a water fountain as he pounds, pumps.

'We cum together?'

'If ya like.'

Morning glory hazard.

30

The two faced bitch comes up running, like shit wouldn't melt in its mouth. 'I hate it when we're not friends.'

'Fuck off.' Pull away from its manipulative embrace.

Then *he* arrives, his face set in stone, sour, bitter, like his voice. 'You can see he got the message, his face gives away that he's been moaning and crying.'

'What?'

'No point lying. When you see the maps and plans don't let them hurt you too much.'

'I don't get it.'

'You will.' Away he goes, off into the distance.

At his home, desk filled with paper, they make no sense at all, covered with cum soiled underwear. Who's been a busy boy then? Used condoms everywhere.

Stand against the door and fall to the knees. Tears, stupid tears falling down stupid face. Why does it still hurt? Maybe that bitter face meant more to me than I realised.

Still invading my dreams, still lingering, mind trying to force you out. Expel you like cancer.

From now on, only let the right one in.

31

Glass syringe placed on top of paper skin.

Stumble; fumble. What a load of hot air.

How can sleep leave you feeling so... I dunno, drained? But then again it was so real, everything coloured in glorious real life colours. What do you have to say for yourself boy? No daddy, please don't hit me. Give me a reason why I shouldn't? Erm… *smack* Ow. You weren't quick enough.

32

Two faced bitch, backstabbing cow. Run, go tell everyone what you overhear and twist it with your venom. Bad mouth me in front of *him*. You leech hanging onto two other leeches because there is nothing else for you to do with your pathetic existence.

As for *you*, what the fuck did you look like? Trying to fit in with their style, you looked like an uncomfortable nob. Yeah, pure nob, stupid scarf wrapped gaily round your neck, the boots you still can't walk in after a year. Haha. Nob.

Surely I'd stop being such a red-hot topic by now. Get over me, you never see me so why does everything satisfy you so much?

'He's bad, got to watch him.' Oh fuck off.

Fuck you.

33

Fuck me, dry ash of a smoker's morning mouth, bitter, cancerous. Dry lips, one little crack. The room so cold it all feels damp. A ghost room, the mist at the end of the bed.

    Huddled against the cold under a duvet. Awake, asleep; awake, asleep. Just wanna stay here. You always hear that, so why can't we? Oh yeah, money. Money is evil. Evil as the morals of a corrupt government.

34

Love, brotherly and/or true. It rests in the eyes, so beautiful to be able to look so deep inside someone. To have so much access to their soul.

I wouldn't change what we have. I'm your dirty little secret at the moment and that makes me smile. Our presence together enough to break the hearts of others, to shatter their hopes, memories and egos.

Fuck, I'm in love. Always have been; always will be. *You. Mine.*

This heart will be broken again by the same person, but so be it.

35

That's what I wanted to happen. The past would never understand the present. That's the way it goes. Don't like it, fuck off.

    Yeah coz you look so happy. Is finding your 'sexual self' making you feel good? Or have you realised what you've lost? I hope it burns when you realise who you lost it to.

36

Devils in the dead of night feasting upon the flesh of the unborn. Diseased creatures rotting in the wombs of expectant mothers, praying dead prayers to silent gods laying sleepily in pits of sordid sin; their cocks throbbing in the cunts of goddesses.

Here lies the death of religion, naked and marked by the scent of sex. Semen splattered walls and sweat drenched sheets. Born from a cunt, live like a cunt, die smelling like a cunt. Sex the scent of mankind.

37

That dream vision, in your mind he's yours. You're fucking every hole in his business.

'Hello mistress, didn't I tell you about the past?'

Mohawk man was obviously mine.

The path of fate. We are all in this position for a reason which will all be made clear soon. Certain chapters of life are coming to their conclusions preparing for the new. The next step is almost here. I can feel it building up. Things will become different.

38

Get out of my head, get out of my head, get out of my motherfucking head.

These dreams are mine, my visions. A place freed from anyone but who I choose. So fuck off.

Shadow man leave, go. This is not your time. Now is not your time. This isn't how I die. I'm gonna be free.

Acid drops dip, corroding away at the world around it. Drip, drip, drip. It's only a matter of time. Everything corrodes, corrupts. Fade to black and roll the end credits.

One hundred ways to cure pain all locked within bottles. A pill for everything. Happy, sad, up or down. Sleep or awake or in between. Back to the Land of Nod.

The sweetest revenge is to continue living.

39

A sea of faces, forbidden and dead. All in a line, wasted and decaying. Waiting for salvation, waiting for the end, waiting for a bus to the Final Judgment.

So many seeds sowed into the earth, doing nothing; too lazy to germinate, too lazy to grow as intended. Dead from the start. Dead from creation. Soulless.

There is no secret that cannot be voiced. There is no lie that cannot be told. There is no hope in useless dreaming.

40

Empty, empty, bled dry. So hollow inside.

41

A photo can say a thousand words but every one of them is in the past. Their moment locked, lost within a memory. Empty and voiceless they cannot be relived.

A photo is a memory of a memory, a ghost of what once was. In some cases, a ghost of a ghost.

42

A road without distance, without directions or landmarks. A blank canvas in front, a splattered paint trail behind, marking where we have been and can never tread again. For one reason we must never turn back and walk where we have been, nothing can change what was, but what was can change what could be. The past is the present's death every second. All three are but a second apart.

Walk forward in the distance unknown and take everything as it comes.

Think, think. Think without regret. Think without remorse or wanting. If you do not know everything, you don't need to know it all. The lies hidden as secrets behind your back need not be revealed for they will only damage what you become.

Die, dead. Rot, rebirth. One tear can save and one can kill.

43

Wet dick from cum, seeping from one eye. Who said anything about it not all coming out?

Pull, tug, yank. However you want to do it the end result is always the same. At least there's no small talk afterwards.

I will leave my taste on your soul. You'll never forget me. For good or bad, I cannot be forgotten.

44

A friend, what makes a friend? Time spent with people and their two bit pathetic attitudes. What do you want? Some juicy bit of gossip for you to stick your leech mouths to? Sucking it dry until you need something new. Lie upon lie. Build up an image of what you want. Who cares if it's true or not. Fuck you. Do what you want. Say whatever keeps you warm inside.

Leeches, parasites. Two faced pieces of shit crawling around in the toilet bowl of life. How pathetic you all look. How meaningless you all sound. You can't hurt me and yet you still think you can. You are the past. I'm living the present whilst looking to the future. Take a running jump off the cliff that is your no hope creations. I'd love to see each one of you fail as much as you're hoping I will.

Two heads arguing upon one shoulder. One hand cuts off the nose to spite a face; another cuts off a lip, an ear, an eye. Killing all the wise monkeys in one motion. Arm fights arm until there is nothing more than a mass of weeping sores for which no one cares. Just put it out with the trash.

Who are you? What are you? Why have you come here to sleep on this side of the bed? Hmm?

45

What thoughts can keep you awake all night? Something hidden deep within the subconscious, niggling away and causing such pointless frustration.

To just be able to close your eyes and vanish must be such a luxury instead of tossing and turning for hours on end in a vain hope of escape.

Dream a dreamless sleep. See no visions of memories, just a void. Empty, black. Dead.

Soulless and vacant this is our destiny. Destiny on a world spinning around. Rotating. Day follows night; night follows day. Constant but never the same. Everything changes, let's lay on our backs and let it happen all around us. As long as the dream remains let this world crumble to ash. Let the abandonment begin.

There is no way in, there never was.

A heckless asparagus.

46

Do you dream to wonder? A tree of steel and ice. A world twisted and burnt, a framework of metal surrounding its dying core. Struggling to survive around faded embers.

One day I could kill you, maybe I already did.

47

Sex is something that controls the future. For every wank a possible life is squirted out onto bare flesh; here it dies, its moment lost, its possibilities ended. Oh well, I'm gay, every time I cum I spit out wasted sperm. All everyone needs is a good fucking.

Mr, you are so crude. Yeah? And?

48

A code, a code, my kingdom for a motherfucking code.

Open your mouth wide and let it all in. Deep throat, break your jaw so you can take it even further. This is what you want right? You won't give me the sex I want, yet you'll suck me off. Go on, gag on it. I'll force it right to the back when I cum, so not only will you choke twice, you'll swallow as well.

Stick a finger up the ass. A bottle; stretch, stretch. Fist. You didn't cum? Oh well, wank. Be quick so I can sleep.

'I was just sick, do you want me to leave?' Actually... yeah.

Fat guy messages. 'Hey wanna fuck?' Reply is too simple, 'If I wanted to fuck a pig I'd go to a farm.'

Uphill mining through a marmite cavern.

49

For fucksake. Stupid me. More than stupid. Pick a card and throw it into the air. A joker spinning towards the sun. Always falling for the ones I can never have. Always feeling let down. Bad fucking apples. I should learn to stay away from fruit. Two bit fuckers.

Lean back and push against, cock slips up ass. Oh yeah, pushed in deep and held. Pound, pound.

Bed springs squeal and squeak. Pull out and flip position.

Squirt against the hole. Rub; push in a little then pull out, fingers up their ass. Slip, slide. Someone gets given a pearl necklace in return.

Look at all the cum on the bed. You chose to that side. Sleep in it.

Did I send them? Yes. Did I receive the message I was replying to? Maybe not. Crack, shatter. Gunk oozing from every corner of the brain. Insanity erupting. Maybe I'm going crazy, maybe that happened years ago. Too many doors left open and now the Otherside is trying to get in. If not in, trying to pull me through.

I don't wanna be on the dark side of the mirror.

50

I guess I'm at that point. The none caring point. The part where everything has truly gone. All past erased like discarded pencil lines. An imprint that is covered with something new. Life eraser. Rub, rub, cum. Shit, was rubbing the wrong part.

'The number you have dialled has not been recognised. Please hang up and try again.'

This was all done. Everything was good. Sorted, planned out and ended. But it was but a dream. Everything is all a dream. Wake up and it's all back to its pitiful existence. Great. Will I ever be free from this hole that I'm in?

Slipping deep, hands clawing at the sides of some beast's throat. This Antichrist's voice is being silenced. No one is listening. No one wants to. Fuck.

So the needle hits the vein. Slipping through the skin as smoothly as a cock up a cunt or lubricated ass. They say you can never cure the addiction, but when reality is like this why would you really want to?

Something snaps. The silent O of the barrel in your throat. One click salvation. Bang. Pop. Blood pours like a waterfall from your nose. So much blood from such a small creature. Lay there on the ground. Twisted. Fragments of who you were. Fragments. The glass man finally shattered. Exploded into billions of tiny pieces. One for every pathetic existence on this miserable blue planet that spins silently towards oblivion.

Click the fingers but never wake. All those pointless suicides escaped into nothing. Nothing at all. Tommy Boy's corpse just hangs from the ceiling as he sits on the bed watching it sway with no escape. Rosie Girl holds the hand of her ODing existence and wonders what the fucking point was.

The dead have nowhere to go and no means of escape. The gates of Heaven are closed, not because it's full but because it never existed. All that is there is a pile of rotting hopes. Shattered and brittle prayers upon which the throne of a brain dead deity sits.

We exist in Hell. There is only Hell. What more could there be?

Then everyone wakes up. It was all a dream. Everything was all a dream and there is nothing but the darkness.

This, whatever *it* is, was just a dream.

BOOK TWO

FIVE NOTES OF SUICIDE

#1

Third of December

So, everyone is allowed their say. Put feelings to paper in an attempt to make them more meaningful. So why do I feel this way? Why did that singular day piss me off? Maybe because it was the first day in ages I could go and spend time with the guy I love without having to worry about anything. I'd been looking forward to it for weeks. So what did I want?

Selfishly just to enjoy myself. Yeah, like that could happen.

It wasn't just the day that was ruined. I'd wanted to go out that night as well. I'd wanted to go out, be myself and get drunk, not having to worry about making a good impression on people or having to get up early the next day for work. Maybe that's stupid but I haven't had a proper night out in ages, let alone with my boyfriend. It was the only chance to do it when we weren't either tired from work or whatever, and it remains the only time until the New Year. Pretty much the only time up until then in general. So, sorry for being selfish and upset.

Does it hurt you're gonna do that with someone else? That you prefer to do it with someone else? Yeah, but only on that selfish level, not a controlling way. I need to let my hair down but don't have the chance, sorry if that gets to me a bit. It just feels nothing is done together anymore. Guess this is the whole together but separate stuff. I'm used to it anyway; it's what my last few boyfriends have done. Too 'ashamed' of stupid me to be seen out with me.

It's how I feel, not saying it's true or not. I'm just a constant disappointment.

[Cigarette break]

Cigarette over, I might as well continue given there's no one around. Just another day with evil thoughts running round my head. Sometimes it feels that my attention is always wanted and I try to give as much as I can, but then when I need it, need some attention to do what I want, it's like I can't get it. I wanna go out - 'can't afford it', 'too busy'. That's all I seem to hear from people and then see them going off and doing what they said they couldn't with other people. One day I'm going to stop asking and no one will ask in return. I know because it's what happened in the past. Maybe today will be that day.

    I wouldn't say all this is about me, but about how people value me. I don't feel valued, just a commodity, there only when you want me. If I say how I feel, I feel stupid. Just moaning, sulking me trying to bring everyone down. The one to blame for everything. If something doesn't go to plan when I'm around then just say it's my fault. Much easier than questioning the rest of the people there. I'll sit there and just take it. It's what I do. How will you manage once I've gone?

I'd be such a good loner, but only if I liked being alone. Being alone is the one thing I fear. The silence is when I get down and listen to the stupid voices in my head. Put me on the shelf and come back to me when you feel the need to. I'll be okay. No I fucking won't and don't send me your stupid 'I'm having so much fun' texts when you know I'm sat around with absolutely nothing to do. How do you think that makes me feel? Oh I forgot; it's never about how *I* feel, only how you all do.

This has become generalised. Talking about the shit in my head. Disposable, discard-able me. What day is rubbish collection?

[Break]

So now I'm sat in the pub with a pint of Strongbow and a cigarette. Ha, sat in a pub alone, I'm getting used to it gradually. Thingy served me today, he served me yesterday, I guess I've become a local now. It's a badly rolled cigarette as well. I hate fresh tobacco.

I don't want to read back through this because I know it's all 'meh', moan, insecure, insecure. But at least it's out of my head. I came in the pub partly because I really needed a drink, and partly because I don't want to go home to an empty house. So a pint wastes a bit of time I guess.

Don't know what to write now.

I AM A GHOST.

One more cigarette then I'll go home. I feel lonely. The one thing I thought, hoped, prayed that moving here would solve.

[Break]

Home now. Tea and biscuits. Welcome. I feel really hollow. Fragile. Like it's me at fault constantly and forever. Put yourself in my place. How would you feel if you were constantly pushed aside, dismissed, ignored? What if the people doing it are meant to be your friends, your family, your boyfriend? Sorry, that's annoyance, not anger. I feel like I'm just slaving away, not seeing any of my money and for what? To have the piss taken. End of the day they'll have more fun without me, just don't do that whole 'would have been better if you was there' crap. Don't do the whole 'it's been ages since we saw you' bullshit. If you'd wanted me there you would of asked.

Meh, this has turned into a stream of my thoughts, just pouring out of my head. Well, I'm glad you've got someone you can get away from it all with. Just spend days filling me with negativity then let me just deal with it. Cheers. What is it? Revenge? Pleasure? So who am I meant to turn to about it? Oh yeah, there's no one. Just file it away in my head and lock it in the filing cabinet.

Argh!! This is why I never let my thoughts speak. They get me down, but what does that matter this one final time?

[Break]

So what if I have a quiet moment, battling shit in my head that I don't want to talk about? Do I need to be forced to speak? Do I need to be made to feel bad because I don't open my mouth? Do I need to hear how my thoughts must be about someone else? No, no, no. Do I need to have my insecurities filled with more? NO. Maybe I just need a hug, some space, some time to sort my stupid head out. Maybe I did. Pretty useless now though.

This is me. This has always been me. The day to day me no one ever sees. Don't you know how much I wish there would be a day when I don't have a negative in my head? I don't need to hear all this 'you can change it if you truly want to' psychobabble. I've tried; it's still the same. Put a gun against my head to silence me. I just want to hear silence.

I guess this sounds like I'm a negative person. I'm not. Guess I'm just a bit 'emo', a bit sensitive and self-conscious. A tortured soul. My arrogance masks an inner soul that has years of put downs, insults and disappointments scarred all over it.

I think that's the best word to use. Disappointment. Things never run like I see them in my head. Constantly disappointed and let down. Nothing ever lives up to my hopes and dreams. Well not 'nothing' because that's a lie. Just my head visions and plans. Sometimes it feels like I'm seeking something I can never have. I'm always trying to reach it; it's just never good enough. I'm never good enough.

Demons; demons everywhere. Scratching with their stupid claws. Feed them with your pretty fears and watch their bellies grow.

Hello silence, hello loneliness, hello self. So what are we going to talk about today?

BANG!!

My feelings only mean something when they don't compromise yours, but guess what. When you read this my feelings won't mean anything because I'll be gone. Exited into the silence. I hope that doesn't inconvenience you too much.

#2

I'm sorry. I'm sorry for your grief but not for what I have done. Please find it in your hearts to forgive me; this was for the best. Believe me, it was my action made by my choice, so I should know.

#3

For the past few days I've felt like shit... like I haven't known what to do with myself... like I'm walking around in limbo. I thought about where I'm going to be in a year's time and what I'm going to be doing and the scary thing was that I hit a blank. I couldn't see anything.

    You turn over in your mind everything, and realise how often you get lied to by society and those that mean so much to you. I don't know if I can take it anymore. I don't know if I can carry on producing award-winning fake smiles and faux-happiness. It's draining me. I'm gradually slowing down. I feel sick for no reason.

Moments of happiness are getting shorter... well it seems that way. I'll be happy then something will knock me off my pedestal and I'll be wallowing in the dirt and nothingness I've become so accustomed to. I just want to rip out of my skin and fly away and be happy... truly happy. To be free from the lies and bullshit.

I feel nothing... empty. I'm done with trust; I'm done with care. Fuck I can't even trust myself anymore. I've fought the blackness for years but it's getting too strong. The man in the shadows is slowly getting ready to show me his face.

This isn't a cry for help... don't think I want or need it. This is a statement of how it is.

I am dirt. I am dirt. I am dirt.

Who knew you could get hurt so many times? There's just been so much shit blasting through my head that I haven't been able to compute it all.

Well, all I want to say is that I dunno. Stupid conclusion to make after the many drug induced soul searches and downers. I mean okay, Saturday I had a really bad trip but throughout it I learnt a few things, namely that no matter how much I wanted to phone them for help, understanding, I knew it would solve nothing, would make matters in my head worse. So I wrote, scribbled it all out in my journal. You imagine a good thing and then you come off and realise that everything is depressingly the same. There's things I need to sort out, okay I guess it's the curse of mankind to not be happy with what he has. I mean why should we be? Spinning round on a ball of distrust, anger and hatred, living our pointless insignificant lives. I once always wanted a family, but now I can't think of anything crueller than creating new life to endure this world of destruction.

Maybe it's because I've achieved everything I aimed to achieve in this life that I feel so empty, like

I'm just here with no purpose at all, moving slowly forward day to day. I've been off my face so many times, seen the way people exist, act, that I have a total disgust for the wage whores working careers they hate just so they can afford to piss away their lives with anything that numbs them. A world where hopes and dreams lay shattered by the wayside. Maybe I wasn't meant for this time. I just can't see the point of merely existing. I've always wanted to have fun, to make a change, to be somebody. Maybe I should grow up, pull my head out of the clouds, but then why should I? If my happiness is pinned only on dreams, then why break the one connection to it that I have? I'd rather end it all now than waste away, knowing that I serve no purpose in the great scheme of things. Then at least I could come back with a clean slate and try again, and if there is no reincarnation, well, that's even better.

I know this sounds lame but I've almost forgotten what it's like to hang out with a group of mates who actually give a fuck about you, who miss you when you're not around, who don't have some hidden motive guiding them.

I've forgotten what it feels like to not see fuck ups in reality, glitches, computer errors, people screaming at me from the corner of my eye.

I've forgotten what it feels like to have a night without nightmares. Every night I awake, clawing and thrashing out. Images rushing through my head; bad images. Every fucking night. So many demons in my head. Conversations, events, people played out in vivid colour, real. I could touch, awake in another dream, another nightmare.

So yeah, at the end of it all, I dunno.

So I sat and thought about everything today and it dragged me so fucking down, too much to try and understand. So what to do? Turn to your best friend. So you send an e-mail as you have no phone credit. You know the score, 'I'm feeling down, need a friend to talk to, wanna meet?'

The reply: 'It's good to hear from you, sorry to hear that you've been down but I will be too busy to meet for the next two weeks or so. If you need advice sooner than that, feel free to email me with whatever's bugging you, and I'll get back to you soon.'

Hmm okay, thanks, cheers. You know it's nice to know that when I put in all the effort to put my friends first none of them return the favour. I guess my feelings and thoughts aren't important enough for their time. After all I did, you would think one afternoon to take my mind off all the shit exploding in my head right now wouldn't be such a chore, that maybe everything would be put down to one side just for *me*.

Maybe I'm asking too much. I mean I'm there for everyone, offering support and help, a shoulder to cry on, but who's there for me? Who puts in the time of day for me? Burden me with your problems but listen to none of mine. Cheers.

Dear agony aunt, I've just swallowed a load of pills, do you think I should wash them down with vodka or turps? Please get back as soon as you can.

You know what, keep your e-mail 'advice-line'.

I'm starting to wonder if I actually exist. I mean no one even acknowledges my presence. None of my so called new friends even try to contact me and when I say 'hi' they're always too busy or just simply ignore me... well, until they have a problem or need to moan about something. I'm like a discarded imaginary friend.

Maybe I've just become too disillusioned with the world and its people. Everyone I meet nowadays only wants to fuck me, and when they realise it's not gonna happen they just stop talking. So there's me left alone, yet again. Oh, I really liked you but now you can't be bothered to give me the time of day. Cheers. And they wonder why I find it hard to trust people.

I guess I'm better on my own. That way I don't have to worry about losing people or being used. That way I don't have to be constantly disappointed by people, there's no broken promises. One day I might actually be able to convince myself I like being alone without anyone caring about my existence. That's what hurts the most. I could disappear off the face of the Earth tomorrow and not be missed. No one would ask questions, no one would wonder where I'd gone. Then in a few years they might say 'anyone know what happened to him? No? Oh never mind then.' I've become a ghost. All I am is a photo on a profile, a voice in a memory, and I can't understand why that is. Am I that bad a person?

In a sense I feel trapped. I know what I want to do but I'm never given the opportunity to do it. Some people get everything; some people get nothing. Some people are just left waiting. I'm tired of waiting, it's like my life has been put on hold whilst I wait in queue to be moved onto the next challenge. I keep getting told that 'something is just round the corner', and whilst that might actually be the case, it's a very long corridor I'm walking down at the moment.

I can't be fucked with this shit. I've had enough. Finally had enough; don't want anymore. At the end of the day, I don't need to worry. I'm not going to here this time tomorrow.

#4

Why do I keep doing this? I mean why can't I just keep my stupid mouth closed and bite the tongue within it, even to the point it bleeds. What good has this shouting done apart from making me a villain again? Always the villain, guess that's the only thing I'm good at.

    I guess it's better for everyone if I just vanish. That way they won't have to put up with all my stupid outbursts. I just see red and 'bang' everything is fucked.

I'm just an embarrassment. It's what I've always been told. Just a pure and simple embarrassment. Fuck. People have their opinions of me. Fuck, they might actually be right. Either way I really should just make my selfish exit from it all. That way I'll stop fucking everyone else's lives up.

I piss on everything that was good like petrol from a can; drop a match and watch it all burn to hell.

I wonder what my ashes would look like.

So, I'm selfish. So, I'm a fuck up. Well, welcome to my most fucked up and selfish act. Do you expect me so write 'Goodbye'? Well guess what? Tough!

Fuck off all of you.

#5

FUCK THIS SHIT!

www.ingramcontent.com/pod-product-compliance
Ingram Content Group UK Ltd.
Pitfield, Milton Keynes, MK11 3LW, UK
UKHW041436180426
11947UKWH00007B/478